Bloom Where You Are Planted

JANE HOFF

Published by Happy Jack Publishing, LLC

Copyright © June 2015

by Jane Hoff

First Printing June 2015

Copyright © 2015 Jane Hoff

All rights reserved.

ISBN: 10: 0692462295

ISBN-13: 978-0692462294

DEDICATION

To my brothers and sisters in Christ who encouraged me to share what they call my "God-given poetry" with others.

CONTENTS

Acknowledgments	i
Part One: Faith & Inspiration	**1**
God Given Poetry	2
Chasing The Wind	3
But We Complicate	4
Goals	5
Climb the Peak	6
Gentle Megaphone	7
It's How	8
Just Because	9
Strings	10
Quite Brand New	11
Stay Aware	12
God's Centerpiece	13
God's In Control	14
I Thank You Holy Spirit	15
Just Ask	16
Maximize the Moment	17
Pruning	18
The Choice	20
The Heart Tuner	21
There's Only One Way to Heaven	22
Today is the Day of Decision	24
Who Will Go	25
A Real Gift	26
Christmas Senses	27
At Last	28
Bloom Where You Are Planted	29
Easter Baskets	30
Emancipation	31
Live Until You Die	32
My Friend	33
Oh, Love Divine	34
Thankful to Belong	35
Thanks, Jesus	36
The Finishing Tool	37

JANE HOFF

The Pious Parrot	38
Two Things I've Learned	39
Vitamin J	40
Fingerprints	41
You	42

Part Two: Family, Reflections & Fun 44

Just Scuffin' Down the Fairway	45
Bud's Feelings	46
Bud in Alzheimer's Unit	48
My Darling Bud	49
Reflections	50
Until We Assume Responsibility	52
Sunshine's Glow	53
I Wish I Had	54
Lingering Essence	56
Music Without a Song	57
The Unknown Pregnancy	58
The Big One	59
Rabbit's Foot	60
The Rental Car	61
Like the Roach	62
City of Palms	63
The Art Critic	64
Things I Hate	65
Dad Used to Say	66
Your Chair is Empty, Daddy	67
His Biggest Fan	68
My Mom	71
Thinking	74
About the Author	75

ACKNOWLEDGMENTS

I'd like to thank everyone who has encouraged me to share my poetry with a wider audience.

PART ONE:
FAITH & INSPIRATION

GOD-GIVEN POETRY

I'm thankful to God
For my poetry
And this chance to share
Which at last I see

So read on, dear ones
And may you enjoy
Lines scribbled by me
Here in Illinois

May 4, 2015

CHASING THE WIND

I chose to chase the wind
And ran and ran and ran
Crossed the shadow of the sunset
Then exhaustion came, unplanned

Tried to wear too many hats
To follow every lead
Learned about priority
To fill the greatest need

I am but only one
Can't spread myself too thin
By sticking to these guidelines
We all are bound to win

September 19, 2009

BUT WE COMPLICATE

Life is quite simple, but we complicate
In our hurry, we detest the wait
And expect God to do things our way
No wonder we go astray
We're like the cart before the horse
And that has never worked, of course

Love surrounds us like the air
His Holy Presence is everywhere
All we need to do is pause
Quiet our soul, which with hunger gnaws
Search for His guidance, obey His will
And let Him help us ascend life's hill

He will reach down with tender touch
Reveal, again, that He cares so much
If only we but give Him time
Relax in His arms, we'll know love sublime
Problems, soon, He will eradicate
If but like a horse, we'll slow our gait

August 25, 1989

GOALS

To grow old, yet not cold
To grow wise, and not surmise
To be warm and do no harm
To be pure and willing to endure
To be kind with an open mind
To do good as I know I should
To be meek, yet not weak
To be humble, and not grumble
To be filled with love, given from above
To experience joy – like a suntanned boy
To know Heavenly peace, which does not cease:
There are my goals

To serve my Savior
I'll watch my behavior
To help my Lord
I'll be in one accord
While on this Earth
I had a second birth
And dedicate my life
To being a better wife
God put me here
To help my dear
Lord, help me to be what he wants of me
This is my ultimate goal

September 20, 1985

CLIMB THE PEAK

Give birth to your potential
Because you are unique
No one can do it like you
Come on now, climb the peak

You started at the base
It was an easy stroll
But as you neared the summit
You craved the crater's bowl

Don't tire now as you're nearing
The point you can attain
Push on, call on endurance
And conquest you will gain

September 26, 1986

GENTLE MEGAPHONE

What did you learn from life?
Do you have a tale to tell?
What should you pass on to others?
Toll out, you townhouse bell

Spread peels of wisdom's gongings
To youthful listening ears
Ring forth eternal truths
Alerting him who hears

Be not dull nor muffled
But sound with vibrant tone
Beckon wandering sheep
Be a gentle megaphone

Teach them lasting principles
In order to carry them through
And then as they grow older
They'll give thanks remembering you

September 26, 1986

IT'S HOW

It's not how gray your hair is
Or how wrinkled is your brow
Or if you're past child-bearing age
Or productive as a cow

It's not how much you know
Whether your vocabulary's big
It's not if you are bald
Or if you wear a wig

It's how you help those strangers
The ones you've never seen
It's how you love those close to you
You know precisely what I mean

It is those sweet, sweet spirits
The kind we know are best
Who make this world a worthwhile place
Where we must pass the test

Jesus became our example
He showed us how to be
Lord, keep our eyes on Him
Let evil from us flee

Oh, we know just how You want us
And we try each day to grow
Into that perfect pattern
Sometimes it seems so slow

May 1, 1986

JUST BECAUSE

Just because I have a
Swimming suit
Doesn't mean that
I can swim
Just because I go to church
Doesn't make me
Close to Him

And though I own
Fine kettles
I'm just a mediocre cook
Who spends much time
On poetry
Upon which few
Will look

But I'm learning
What's important
As my hair is turning white
And am growing closer to
The Lord
As the end comes near in sight

I thank my
God each day
For our Savior who arose
And plan to be ready
When my life comes to
A close

December 28, 1986

STRINGS

Before I knew Jesus
Or of how He cares for me
I hung to this life
Quite precariously

The string to which I held
Grew weaker every day
Then I gave my life to God
Saying, "Do with me as You may."

And now, I don't hold on
Instead, God's holding me
By His iron string of faith
There is security

No matter what's ahead
The bliss or trials of life
The roses or the thorns
The happiness or strife

I know my Loved One
Who has known me from the start
Will be my help and guide
For He lives here in my heart

His Promise – never to leave me
I've seen Him keep each day
And am thankful for the ribbon
That ties us when I pray

The string of faith – unbroken
Is stronger than a chain
With such a mighty tool
New life, you, too, can gain

August 12, 1987

QUITE BRAND NEW

God didn't just refurbish me
He made me quite brand new
Now since His spirit is my guide
I've changed my point of view

Before, I muddled through each day
And sought for worldly gain
Pretending life was only now
To please me was my aim

If you choose Him for your Savior
He will change you too
Then you will want to share His love
In all the things you do

August 7, 2013

STAY AWARE

After a long, drawn-out winter
A butterfly fluttered by
The wee insect intrigued me
As its brilliance caught my eye

Then realization came:
God had made that lovely thing
Just as He made you and me
Which caused my heart to stop and sing

I am thankful I know Him
That He cares so much for us
It's amazing that He does
And with no apparent fuss!

Be certain to stay aware
There are sparkles every day
Merely stop, look, and listen
Never let them slip away

March 31, 2015

GOD'S CENTERPIECE

Each tiny, pretty flower
Has beauty of its own
Until arranged by skillful hand
Its splendor is unknown

But when a group of flowers
Are placed with expertise
No longer does each stand as one
But blends into the piece

The same is true of people
The members of a church
When God draws them together
No longer do they search

They fit together perfectly
And like a fine bouquet
Their unity is seen by all
Without communique

November 15, 1995

GOD'S IN CONTROL

The change didn't happen overnight
For I put up my usual fight
Yet God persuaded me: persevere
And face tough trials without fear

It was from the Spirit I would learn
That troubles are God's; not my concern
Now I step aside and simply wait
For His help with Satan's bait

If I quit trying to run the show
And allow God complete control
Stop spinning my wheels and just rest,
As always, God knows what is best

August 8, 2014

I THANK YOU, HOLY SPIRIT

Holy Spirit, will You be there
If I attain the goal?
I've read of the Father and the Son
But the three of You are whole

Or are You just to be on Earth
To help us while we're here?
In case I never meet You
I'll thank You while You're near

Patiently You've guided
And taught me right from wrong
Thanks for ever being there
When anything went wrong

You've helped to keep me silent
You've helped me speak when should
You've given gifts to this pitiful soul
Which only a Father could

I thank You for Your presence
For remaining when He left
For never giving up on me
And having room in Your heart's cleft

December 21, 1988

JUST ASK

When you don't know where to turn
And nothing seems to go right
Fix your eyes on the Lord above
And then keep Him in your sight

When you don't know what to do
And things are going wrong
Ask the One who can solve it all
He would have helped you all along

July 1982

MAXIMIZE THE MOMENT

Maximize the moment
Don't let it slip away
Savor all your seconds
Right now and through the day

Don't waste a wee instant
Appreciate it all
From the brilliant sunrise
To the cardinal's call

Constantly be aware
Of every breath you take
Inhale the gift of life
God-given for your sake

Both in bad and good times
God's forever by your side
The best thing you can do:
Be wise and let Him guide

Life will go much smoother
In every single way
And you will be so glad
You had the time to pray

Maximize the moment
In everything you do
Realization comes:
God's love is blessing you

April 6, 2014

PRUNING

The first time that I pruned
It was so hard on me
For from a little twig
It had grown to be a tree

My shears so sharp and shiny
Like a weapon in my hand
Looked ever so foreboding
Cut away – I understand

It pressed my soul
To squeeze that handle
So a few I left unsheared
So I became a vandal

I stole the very life from those
Whose correction I failed to yield
And like a parent too lax to correct
Left a wild thing in that field

Later I beheld those altered branches
Abundantly they grew
The others weren't so healthy
And then at last I knew

I need to do some pruning;
This time to look at me
God, nip away
So I can grow abundantly

How can I grow in a holy life
If I don't see what is wrong?
My prayer is, God keep pruning me
Make me not a sounding gong

Give me wisdom to look inward
Help me know just where to trim
And then, to see with Your help
That You'll fill me to the brim

March 31, 1986

THE CHOICE

With Your all-encompassing love
Your Kingdom is ruled on high
And Your scepter, like pointed finger
Reaches to us from the sky

And it, Your Holy Spirit
Becomes a beckoning tool
Those who have felt this power
Are joyously under Your rule

But people who will not submit
Who rebelliously do their own thing
May, perhaps, unknowingly
Have Satan for their king

For we must belong to one;
No one belongs to two
Satan confuses our minds
But the choice is he or You

January 16, 1990

THE HEART TUNER

Gently He knocked, then
Opened my hidden door
His tap was recognized
Yes, I'd heard it times before

But today I let Him in
Knowing my heart was out of tune
And thankfully gave to Him
For He had come – none too soon

As He opened His tuning bag
Out of it poured love
And my heartstrings readjusted
Miraculous! – From above

Some of them have weaknesses
Yet, some of them are strong
Now since the tuner lives with me
I know what's right from wrong

Any fine instrument
Is worthless if off key
But brings joy to its owner
When creating harmony

I now belong to You
And know, to You, I'm dear
Help me be a Stradivarius
Sweetly helping others hear

December 26, 1986

THERE'S ONLY ONE WAY TO HEAVEN

There's only one way to Heaven:
You must be born again
Which is your spiritual birth
God's crucial gift to men
You'll feel someone is calling
Though you may not know who
It's God's Holy Spirit
He's motioning to you
You'll realize the reason
He's calling out your name
And when you answer His call
You'll never be the same

There's only one way to Heaven:
When you accept the Lord
He'll be your God and Savior
With unity restored
Then you'll want His forgiveness
For all of your old sin
So unto God confess them
Repentance will begin
Christ can give you the power
To overcome all sin
But be prepared for Satan
He thrives on sneaking in

There's only one way to Heaven:
You will not lose your way
The Spirit lives inside you
And guides you night and day
God gave to all His Scripture
To teach us right from wrong
By following His guidelines
The weak become the strong

Praise God for all His patience
His mercy and His grace
Look forward to the day when
We'll meet Him face to face

October 16, 2012

JANE HOFF

TODAY IS THE DAY OF DECISION

Today is the day of decision
The choice is up to you
I've tried to reach you before
I never could get through

I tried to hold you closely
You pulled back from My care
And even now you seem to think
This is some kind of dare

Tomorrow may be too late
That choice is up to Me
I say this not to frighten you
But to win your soul, you see

Come kneel now in repentance
And cast your sins on Me
I died to save mankind
And set the Spirit free

December 11, 1989-February 9, 1996

WHO WILL GO

Who will go and till My soil
The fertile hearts of men?
Who will teach them of My Word
And convict them of their sin?

Who of you is true and brave
Yet at the same time meek?
Who will go and teach the world?
You are the ones I seek

May 7, 1986

A REAL GIFT

'Twas the night before – 12-24
And all of the songs had been sung
Reminding the mind of old former times
When stockings and custom were hung

Then deep in the heart, there came a stirring
As never had stirred before
St. Nicholas left and Jesus came in
Gentlemanly op'ning the door

And as Jesus came back into Christmas
He'd really been there all the time
The wrapping and presents weren't important
And really seemed sort of a crime

For they'd mocked the real meaning of Christmas
The true gift was given to us
And instead of receiving Love's own gift
We'd been fooled and plagued by the fuss

If the message of Christmas would scatter
During every day of the year
It would shine like the star of Bethlehem
Bringing light to man and good cheer

So the next time you open a present
Think of what a real gift would be
Forgiveness, acceptance, unfailing love
No money could buy all these three.

December 24, 1988

CHRISTMAS SENSES

My nose knows it is Christmas time
The fragrances abound
From pine cones on the tablecloth
To candles burning 'round

My eyes know it is Christmas time
The glitter fills the town
As lights flow from the roof to walk
While scamp'ring up and down

My ears know it is Christmas time
The carols softly play
While ho hos from store Santa Claus
Continue night and day

My mouth knows it is Christmas time
I smack my lips and praise
The fruitcake and the cookie bars
Their numbers do amaze

My touch knows it is Christmas time
Though I am far from home
My loved ones reach through memory
From which they'll never roam

My heart knows it is Christmas time
But does it make real sense
To leave Christ in the background? No –
It makes the purpose dense

He came not just for Christmas time
He came to die for all
He gave His life that we might live
Be sure to hear His call

December 14, 1997

AT LAST

I always thought I had the will
If I put my mind to it
To overcome most anything
If I'd work hard and not quit

For years I tried to change my life
But failed so miserably
Then revelation came at last
It wasn't up to me

When I was born again
Jesus came to live with me
He's making changes in my life
The old me's gone. At last I'm free

Whenever help is needed
And my mind begins to stew
The Holy Spirit guides my thought
In deciding what to do

Praise God for the help He gives
Praise God for Jesus lives

Dedicated to Pastor Jeff Hemken
May 1, 2010

BLOOM WHERE YOU ARE PLANTED

At times we have to make a move
Although not what we want
Quite similar to playing ball
Sometimes we have to bunt

Yes, we'd like to make a "home run"
But that is not our fate
So plant your feet and make a stance
You're now at your home plate

Time to bloom where you are planted
No matter where that be
The heartland of America
Or near a scenic sea

Then as you bloom, may others see
The flowering of your face
You'll soon discover happiness
And joy in your new place

For Ron, Elaine, Tyler, and Devan
July 27, 2013

EASTER BASKETS

Peek beneath the bushes
Look among the flowers
Easter eggs appear
Even in the bowers

Only by exploring
Will the prize be found
And the more you look
The more you'll find around

That's also true of a Christian life
Continue in your quest
Hunt the rare treasures
Until you find what's best

But pretend you know it all
And fail to learn each day
Don't search out the Scriptures
To see what God would say

Then you'll miss His gems of wisdom
Not know what you could be
You'll be an old Easter basket
Cold, bare, empty

May 5, 1997

EMANCIPATION

If you were chained and in slavery
Longing to see the day you'd be free
Tired of your trials and weary within
Perhaps unaware of how you had sinned
And someone came and offered the key
That would loose you for eternity
Would your head shake and you say, "No,
keep the key – to Hell I'll go."

Or would you release yourself to God's love
Free to prepare for Heaven above?
Abolished from sin, no longer in jail
Knowing that Jesus had gone your bail
Living in light, loosed from the past
Darkness then gone from you at last
Smiling with confidence, love in your heart
With God's help you can make a new start

October 19, 1986

LIVE UNTIL YOU DIE

No matter what trials you face
Rely on God's unfailing grace
Recall the unexpected ways
He solved your problems all these days

There may be more you must endure
The future's scary and unsure
But just relax and trust in Him
He'll never leave you on a limb

Yes, live, live, live until you die
A life that's pleasing to the Lord
Then spend eternity with Him
Where you will be in one accord

December 8, 2014

MY FRIEND

I have a friend I'd like you to know
His name is Lord Jesus, and even though
You can't see His face nor grab hold of His hand
He's eternally with me, the way that He planned
He lives in my heart and is changing me
For the better, I hope you can see
That when I listen and heed His voice
It's not difficult to make the right choice
When I read His Bible, things are plain to see
Come meet my Savior; follow Him with me
Together we'll learn what He wants us to do
And by following Him, can start life anew

October 19, 1986

OH, LOVE DIVINE

Oh, love divine, love so precious
Bestowed on us by Lord Jesus
It was He who saved us from sin
Then sent the Spirit to come in

The Spirit's our guide and teacher
And our own internal preacher
We must wait for wisdom from God
And receive His heavenly nod

Then we'll succeed in all we do
For it was His plan we followed through
Oh love divine, love so precious
Thank you Spirit, God, and Jesus

April 7, 2014

THANKFUL TO BELONG

Remember when kids picked their teams:
You waited patiently
And if your name did not get called
'Twas a real catastrophe!

Then when in high school at the prom
You sat with all the girls
The boys strolled by and sized you up:
A swine among the pearls

In spite of all these hurtful things
They never got you down
I bet you tried to pass it off
By acting like a clown

The years went by and now you're grown
You've joined the Christian team
For God chose you to be His child
Your life He will redeem

And, oh, what joy has filled your soul
For though you had done wrong
You're now forgiven of your sins
And thankful to belong

February 19, 2005

THANKS, JESUS

Thanks for giving the choice of second birth
That valuable gift of priceless worth
Without it, I'd still be among the lost
We followers know there is a cost

When we gained the new life, there was much change
And our actions started to rearrange
Before, we thought mainly about self
Sometimes of sinful pleasure, or of wealth

Now we try to be of help to others
To treat them as dear sisters and brothers
We give thanks to you, Lord Jesus, again
For eternal life and forgiving sin

June 26, 2014

THE FINISHING TOOL

God owns a tool called a "finishing tool"
That only skilled craftsmen can use
Sometimes there are hardships
And sorrow and pain
But I know
That all things
From Him
Will bring gain

He formed me and molded
With the greatest of care
Watching my growth
Though I was unaware
He chiseled and shaved
The excess from me
And is using that tool
To make me what I should be

June 20, 1989

THE PIOUS PARROT

So you're a Christian!
Well, isn't that neat?
Go to church on Sunday
Sit in the same seat?

Fold your hands piously
Parroting a prayer
And then come out
Feeling glad you were there?

Stepped back into the world
Weren't changed a bit
If this happened to you
Just emotions were lit

But, if truly converted
You'll try Christ-like to be
He'll shine through you
For others to see

June 17, 1986

TWO THINGS I'VE LEARNED

It took eighty-eight years to learn
All things happen for a reason
Sometimes we can't understand why
Yet everything has its season

Next, there is no coincidence
Things don't magically fall into place
God, who designed the master plan
Directs it with His loving grace

March 26, 2015

VITAMIN J

I took vitamins A, B, C, D and E
And ate all the foods that were good for me
My body was healthy as it could be
But, oh, my mind and soul – oh my
Mind and soul – were botherin' me

And then Lord Jesus spoke to me
And said, "Dear one, can't you see?
I'll feed your soul with vitamin J
Then everything will be o.k.

You can't get it at a drugstore
It's not at the supermart
The only way to obtain it
Is allow me into your heart."

Thank you, Lord, for vitamin J
Now I read the Good Book every day
My body is healthy as it can be
And my mind and soul quit botherin' me

Thank you, Lord, for vitamin J

March 1982

FINGERPRINTS

Fingerprints paint the hall
Revealing their owner's name
Whether with peanut butter or ink
The result is till the same

So how can man in his wisdom
Fail to identify
The Sculptor of the Earth
My question is merely, "Why?"

Why can't we see the Creator
His fingerprints are there
Instead we roam His earth
Without praise. Now is that fair?

Thereby we miss His blessings
And fail to appreciate
The love bestowed on us
Oh Man! – life's more than fate

August 30, 1989

YOU

You, who turns the shower on
The One who shuts them off
You who caused the wind to blow
Perhaps, by just Your cough
You who paint me pictures
Across Your heavenly throne
You, like breath, are with me
I give thanks, I'm not alone

You are here to help me
And give guidance for my way
With expanding heart, I love You
Please listen as I pray

My words of praise are given
And how they humble me
For I meditate Your magnitude
And Your holiness, so pure
Then ponder of Your power
Which ever will endure;
And then I look at me

While next I try to thank You
For the gifts You have bestowed
The list is almost endless
You give, who never owed

And then come my petitions
Which are rattled off with ease
Constantly asking of You –
No time for bended knees

Perhaps if You weren't so available
Perhaps if You weren't so kind
Or if You weren't so generous
I'd keep <u>You</u> more in mind

BLOOM WHERE YOU ARE PLANTED

I love You, Lord, in my own way
And pray You'll help me grow
To be changed into Your image
Like a gardener, apply Your hoe
Please make me more considerate
To help my fellow man
I'll try to be Your servant
In any way I can

December 2-4, 1986

PART TWO:
FAMILY, REFLECTIONS & FUN

JUST SCUFFIN' DOWN THE FAIRWAY

I was scuffin' down the fairway
And try'n to make a rhyme
When my husband shook his head
And said, "It's not the time
To write your little ditties
Or have your fun with words

"No wonder that your golf game
Is flighty as the birds
Now give some concentration
On what you're here to do
Be careful, dear, don't stumble
You're standing on my shoe."

May 27, 1987

BUD'S FEELINGS

The sun is overheated
Mother Nature cut the deal
My eyes fill up with stinging sweat
I'll tell you how I feel

Beginning back in April
I disked and planted corn
Then quicker than a click
It's gone this August morn'

The icy wind swished in
With no mercy, bashed the barn
While crystal shot came pelting
Why did I choose to farm?

No money for insurance
No protection for this loss
For independence, yes, I farm
Yet am I truly boss?

How can I feed the family?
We gamblers need a school
This time the bank takes over
You know the silver rule

We've had some good years here
And, yes, we've had some bad
Big City you are callin' me
But your beckoning is sad

BLOOM WHERE YOU ARE PLANTED

At least there in the city
I'll earn some steady pay
Planning for retirement
And moving home someday

May 7, 1986-February 9, 1996

JANE HOFF

BUD IN ALZHEIMERS UNIT

I walk among the living dead
Whose vacant eyes bore into me
When recognition fails, they stare
Then sink into their savage sea

Wildly I search. There's no lifeline
A rescue I cannot make
The sand sucks at my helpless feet
I, too, am caught; there's no escape

But in our lives hereafter
As all things, these will change
And in the twinkling of an eye
We, too, will rearrange

March 31, 2011

MY DARLING BUD

No longer in person, mere photograph
Causes my gulp as I view your dear face
The hunger is constant; I'm almost starved
And desperately crave your love, embrace

Thanks for the memories you left behind
Those sixty-seven short years of marriage
Although some of them were not filled with bliss
We left the world fantastic lineage

July 23, 2014

REFLECTIONS

Why was my brother bitter
Who could not drink his fill?
He laughed and socialized
And drank 'til he got ill
What seed was planted in him
That molded there and died?
No doctor could discover
The things he tried to hide

There was an outward happiness
Slate eyes reflected pain
With a little squint from sunshine
The corners seared in lanes
I long to look into those eyes
To see his smile as he hugs me
Memories flash psychedelically
Through them once more I see

Had the doctor found the cause
That pickled every cell
My kin would now be with me
And once more he'd be well
We all suspected World War II
Though he had no battle scars
One drink would start him talking
He was known in all the bars

He talked of Mindanao,
The Philippines, New Guinea –
Of ack ack guns and submarines
The Aussies, and a girl named Ginny
Of men who lost their minds
Of some who stayed o'erseas
Of jungle rot; he had no cot
The camp was filled with fleas

The war changed my brother
It made rich men richer
They never even knew his name
Now do you get the picture?

February 26, 1986

UNTIL WE ASSUME RESPONSIBILITY

We're aware of wife and child abuse
It has happened to our friends
Few recognize ecology's rape
Less even try to make amends

Human bruises fade in time
Yet their minds retain the hurt
There are other things can't be restored
For instance: water, air and dirt

And ladies think, "Oh that little bit
Sprayed on my hair,
Won't disturb the ozone."
Yet, they cover their eyes with care

The man hauls out his chemicals
The pests he will defeat
A little in each cow's food
Is detected in the meat

Until we each assume
Responsibility
Of not abusing God-given things
I'll blame you and you blame me

November 7, 1989

SUNSHINE'S GLOW

It was the glow from sunshine
Upon a mound of snow
That caused anticipation
And set my heart aglow

The winter had been torture
It seemed to have no end
And yet the blessed sunshine
Vowed spring was 'round the bend

My frozen mood began to thaw
New life was there to face
As cabin fever melted
A smile was left in place

February 18-March 22, 2014

I WISH I HAD

The crazed hands of my mother
Held the quilting piece taut
Quite deftly wiggling in and out
The needle led the thread
And with the skill of patience
Made a masterpiece for my bed

The State Fair was approaching
For man and beast to show
Their skills and perfections
Things lined up row by row

My momma's quilt won first place
You should have heard us shout!
Then many years later
My children wore it out

At first I was reluctant
To let them use that prize
Momma said, "It's no good
If never seen by eyes.

"Let those little ones enjoy it
While on the floor they play
Perhaps they'll remember
Their old Grandma that way."

Both she and the quilt are gone now
I can't recall her face
But clearly see her hands
Put piece by piece in place

'Twas Grandma's Flower Garden
The colors, every hue
Mom, tears roll down my face
I'd love to talk to you

Somehow I never thanked you
For all you did for us
You met more than our needs
And never made a fuss

Mom, I am feeling lonesome
And miss you oh so much
I wish I had a little scrap
From that quilt so fair
And somehow I had taken time
To show how much I care

In memory of my mother, Nora Vandever
January 29, 1988

LINGERING ESSENCE

She was a tiny elegant package
On whom a bow would have been superfluous
About her hung the air of Texas-rich
Among that swarm of human busyness

He walked by, and you could smell oil
Texas oil, that is – with its sweet fragrance
That lingering essence of fossilized coal
Surrounded him with bold assurance

Her soft brown suit, neatly trimmed in black
Classily displayed her firm, disciplined body
Nose toward ceiling, she condescended, "Hell-ooo."
Dressed in my best, I felt so dowdy

As they sashayed away from me
I received some valuable wisdom
Our attitudes are emitted from us
From deep inside they come

February 24, 1986

MUSIC WITHOUT A SONG

I haven't written a poem for so long
I feel like music without a song
My hands, tired of cooking and cleaning
Desire my brain to do some gleaning

So I'll sit down with fuzzy head
And hope my hand creates instead
You thoughts can come so easily
While other times you seem to flee

There's fun in finding a buried gem
Yet poems, like prayers, need an amen
Yes, poetry, too has a place to quit
And like cousin puzzle, has to fit

Now shaky pen, your point was made
Don't nag at them – just gently fade
First place your plea upon the paper
Then go lie down 'til your next caper

November 4, 1986

THE UNKNOWN PREGNANCY

Little poem, from where did you come?
My pen is like a womb
Delivered of a pregnancy

Little poem, thank you
You've given me great pleasure
Let's hope that there'll be others
These words will also treasure

Little poem don't leave me
For then I'd be depressed
Be my constant companion
Supple at my breast

Then like a chromosome
You'll split in two
Making seed for another
To take the place of you

September 11, 1986

THE BIG ONE

Skipping through the shadows
That lie upon the grass
Emerging in the sunshine
Where he'll sit and bask
Goes the carefree farm boy
With bobbing fishing pole
Dreaming of the big one
Down at the fishing hole

Hours later, now, we see him
As he plods beneath the trees
Thinking of his chores ahead
Absorbing nature's breeze
Thankful for the time he's had
To dive and skinny dip
But once again that tricky whale
Has wiggled from his grip

July 2, 1986

RABBIT'S FOOT

The pumpkin got frosted last night
Lettuce wilted, while not in the pan
The veggies turned brown
Their faces turned down
And now there is nothing to can

The rabbit perked up his long ears
Sensing man; his greatest of fears
The gunshot disturbed
Like an ill-spoken word
So he ran and he ran and he ran

The man cussed out his new toy
Reverting to being a boy
The weapon was blamed
For no animal maimed
Brought me joy, brought me joy, brought me joy!

For though I had tried to outsmart
That rabbit, with fleet-beating heart
I really was glad that an abundance I'd had –
Even though he had tried to annoy

And now he can hide in my woods
And winter it out in the snow
Nature, take care of that poor little hare
'Til he can feast on things that I grow

December 25, 1988

THE RENTAL CAR

After landing at the airport
And unable to find a ride
A rental car seemed the solution
Problems started, I confide

The driver brought the car in front
He spoke but only Spanish
When we tried to question him
He looked at us with anguish

"Where is this?" and "what is that?"
Received the same reply
He answered, "Si" to everything
What use was it to try?

At first we couldn't figure out
The locks – to our chagrin
The driver's seat refused to budge
We sat with knees to chin

I screamed, "What are those flashing lights?"
Bud snapped, "Well, I don't know!"
He turned the knobs and spun the dials
While wipers doe-see-doe

And then we pressed a hidden switch
The sirens shrieked, "Alarm!"
We worked in vain to cut them off
No way would they disarm

So many buttons – which to choose?
I'm sure we tried them all
It wasn't 'til the airbags popped
Was 911 we'd call

December 19, 1995

LIKE THE ROACH

Like the roach who
Succumbed to lethal spray
I'll lie on my back
And look up some day

I hope the embalmer
Does a better job on me
So my feet don't
Stick up for all to see

My feet, you see, are a real big size
And maybe there are some don't realize
So I'd hate to lie within my box
With people laughing at my sox

May 1, 1987

CITY OF PALMS

You funny inverted green mop
So stuck up, with head in the sky
With giant fans aflutter
Are you waving to me a goodbye?

From the upstairs condo window
I bid fond farewell to friend palm
He stands like a guard day and night
Yet bends now with gallant salaam

So long, dear palm. Stay with the cane
Keeping yourselves warm and dry
While Mexican doodads and Texas
Fruit to the frozen North, I must fly

What joy to visit The Valley
Immersed in the warm Texas sunnies
Though my arthritic pains submerged
It's up North I make my monies

Bronchitis will be at the airport
I'm his pick every year
Though I'd like to escape his clutches
It's his wracking cough I fear

To nest in the City of Palms
I'd gladly be a black grackle
Then health and pep would be restored
To this poor hypochondriacal

In Heaven there must be palm trees
Where winters are never cold
With smooth skin and fast gait restored
I'd find no cause to grow old

February 20, 1986

THE ART CRITIC

"Man, you really messed up that one!"

"Which one, honey?"

"The one with the hole in it."

The three-year old was standing
Hands on hips
In the studio
Looking at her
Grandfather's palette

His wife had wanted to hang it
She thought it one of his better paintings
But, then, she was a poet –
And you know how they are

November 29, 1989

THINGS I HATE

I hate canceled flights
When my baby girl's coming home
I hate that slapped-down feeling
Like a dog deprived of bone

I pace about the room
Trying not to bite my lip
But like a German submarine
Someone sank my ship

The Jack-in-the-box failed to pop out
The snow ice cream is bitter
Like Momma cat who prowled all night
I'm missing one of my litter

I hate that she had four days off
And planned a welcomed spree
Then old man winter shook his mop
Keepin' my darling from me

She'll sit by a fire in Virginia
And probably read a good book
While I'll be here in the Midwest
Just a floundering fish on a hook

The food I prepared now sits here
While cold warms, hot grows cold
All of us hate disappointment
But it's worse when you get old

January 22, 1987
For Hannah Hoff Parr

DAD USED TO SAY

If he was found in bed
During the day
Uncharacteristic –
Shamefaced, he'd say

"Me, taking a nap? Don't
You realize
I am in here, merely
Resting my eyes."

January 20, 2015

YOUR CHAIR IS EMPTY, DADDY

Your chair is empty, Daddy
And it makes me feel so sad
I think about the fun
The good times and the bad

But it's so hard at Christmas
To fill my heart with cheer
When there's that vacant space
I wish that you were here

Mommie doesn't say much
Her tears are shed alone
Though I do not see them
It's on her face they're shown

I wish that this was last year
When our family was complete
For Daddy there can never be
A replacement for your seat

December 20, 1988

HIS BIGGEST FAN

In all the years I knew him
There was only once he did something
I didn't like:
He died!

Before that, he never disappointed me
When I needed advice, he was there
When they threw the rice, he was there

My daddy had such a pleasant way about him – so kind
And if ever one had Christian characteristics
The way they are to be
It was he

He loved his family and was loyally devoted to us
We came first – bar nothing, here on earth
He loved his Heavenly Father and was completely sincere
In worshipping Him

At Daddy's funeral, the preacher said that few would
Ever know how many people Daddy had helped
But that was his way – to keep such things quiet

Daddy was a teetotaler, and yet, he was far from a prude
The only time I ever heard him curse
Was when he was hospitalized and had been given drugs
My, was I surprised. What a vocabulary was his

I was his perfect audience
Because I lacked the ability of remembering jokes
He was redundant
But my poor Mother was unfortunate enough
To never forget a thing

He always tried to make every situation cheerful
Even at my mother's funeral – not out of disrespect to her
Nor from trying to hide his grief – but purely to help me through it
He cracked a joke right there as we were seated at the graveside
And I quickly disguised my laugh with a cough
And then he squeezed my hand and we cried

He was a lawyer who practiced for over fifty years
And yet, no one I ever knew hated an argument more than he
He pleaded his cases, which was much more effective,
And he was fair

There was never a doubt of what he expected from those around him
And we gladly worked to fulfill those desires

I was the apple of his eye
And the boundless love could be seen there
His smile was slow and steady
His hair was gorgeous white
He said "Yip, yip," in his sleep
And made up horse stories at night

He taught me prudence and pleasure
Never once did he spank me; Mom got that job
He was a teacher from the heart
Who held me on his knee
And made me feel important
Through his humility

I knew the town respected this man who I called "Dad"
His memory is now reflected
My, he made me glad

We used to go on walks
Particularly when it rained
Under the old umbrella
We'd duck beneath the trees
As he'd sing some ancient ditty
About a peg-legged man

And he knew – my dear, sweet Daddy
That I was his biggest fan

January 27, 1988

MY MOM

My mom ate the necks and backs
And I thought she had odd taste
My mom worked like a whirling dervish
And did everything in haste

My mom scraped the pans so long that
The clanging got on your nerves
My mom drove the car so slowly
Particularly 'round curves

My mom fed the hungry bums
'Twas on the back steps
After they were gone
I've seen how hard she wept

She nagged my dad
I never knew why
She did it until
The day she died

Her grammar was poor
And she sweated a lot
Kitchens and laundries
Were sweltering hot

She hummed religious tunes
Whenever she got upset
The louder she hummed, the more
You knew you'd better get

More than anyone
I've ever known
She hated waste –
A true disgrace

My mom could stitch a frayed collar
'Til it looked brand new
My mom could re-style brother's trousers
Into a skirt, and I've had quite a few

She had me late in life
She could hardly spell
Even as a child, I wrote for her
She said, "You do it so well."

I'm now fifty-nine and it took all these years to realize
My mom never ate white meat until we kids were grown
Then she'd go to an elegant restaurant
One which she easily could own

We laughed behind her back as she stuffed her big, black purse
With bread for the birds, bones for the dog – the original doggie bag –
Sometimes, something for her
This is no gag

I've seen her even wrap up applesauce
"Oh," you must be saying, "now that's carrying things a bit too far."
And I would gently reply, "That depends on
Where you've been and where you are."

My mom had to quit school and start working in
Rich people's homes when she was nine-years old
She never forgot a face or a name and remembered even
Unimportant things, long ago told

She liked to bet on horses!
Now isn't that out of line?
And we all played pinochle
To have a big time

Days were sweet and simple
Work was hard and honest
Mothers always were at home
Nights were always longest

She could make a pan of cinnamon rolls
So quickly you would not believe it
The aroma beckoned us from the porch
Then we'd go to the kitchen and eat

I've eaten so much raw dough
I really should have worms
I always was a sickly child
And picked up lots of germs

My mother was a tender nurse
She knew just how to pat me
And when to switch the cool washcloth
Or bring me toast and tea

January 23, 1986

THINKING

Thinking is so hard
Thinking takes some time
Thinking is productive
Thinking made this rhyme

Thinking hard is better
Thinking slowly, wise
Thinking what to name this poem
Made me cross my eyes

May 4, 1987

ABOUT THE AUTHOR

Jane Hoff attended Northwestern University, then taught grade school for several years. She is a mother of five, with two daughters waiting for her in Heaven. Her three sons live nearby. Although she currently lives in Illinois, Jane has also lived in Missouri, Virginia, and Texas.

At eighty-eight years old, Jane has been writing poetry for more than fifty years. The poems in this book are some of her favorites.

Jane would love to hear from readers. You can contact her through her publisher at happyjackpublishing@gmail.com.

www.ingramcontent.com/pod-product-compliance
Lightning Source LLC
Chambersburg PA
CBHW071330040426
42444CB00009B/2123